*"It is a good thing
to give thanks
unto the Lord."*

—PSALM 92:1.

Thank You, God, for Fall

By Jane Belk Moncure
Illustrated by Frances Hook

THE CHILD'S WORLD ELGIN, ILLINOIS 60120

Library of Congress Cataloging in Publication Data

Moncure, Jane Belk.
  Thank you, God, for fall.

  (The Four seasons)
  Published in 1975 under title: Fall is here!
  SUMMARY: Thanks God, in rhyme, for the various
activities and changes associated with fall.
  [1. Fall—Fiction. 2. Christian life—Fiction.
3. Stores in rhyme] I. Hook, Frances. II. Title.
III. Series.
PZ8.3.M72Th 1979   [E]   79-10030
ISBN 0-89565-081-9

Distributed by Standard Publishing, 8121 Hamilton Avenue,
Cincinnati, Ohio 45231.

PICTURE WORDS

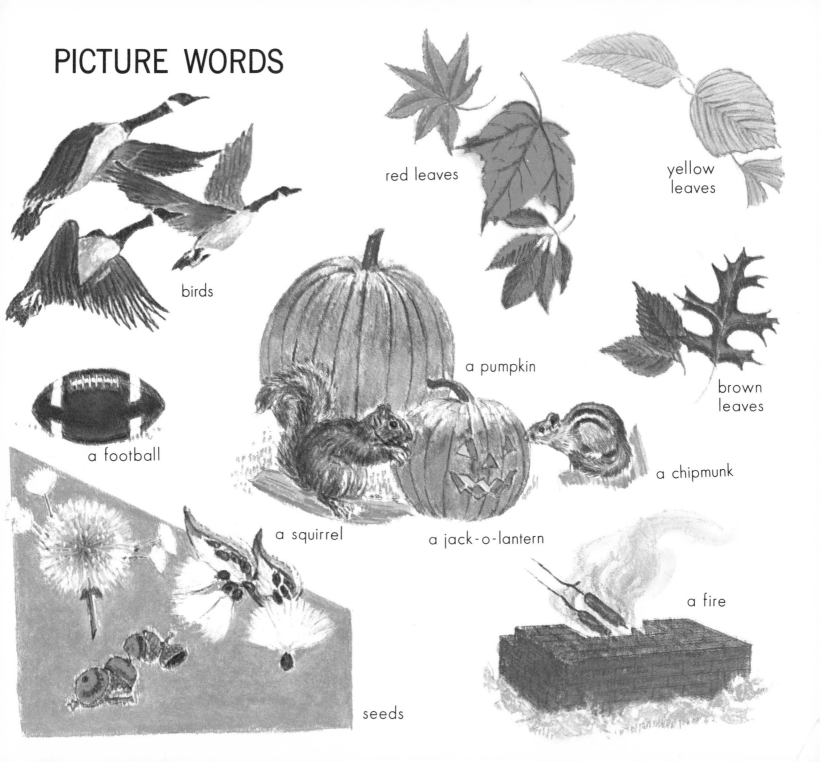

birds

red leaves

yellow leaves

a pumpkin

brown leaves

a football

a squirrel

a jack-o-lantern

a chipmunk

seeds

a fire

Thank You, God, for a fine fall day
when we can run and jump and play.
Thank You, God, for a friend today.

5

Thank You, God, for the world in fall,
for the leaves,
   all yellow
      and orange
      and brown.
I pretend I'm a leaf. I twirl around.
I twirl around and then fall down.

Thank You, God, for my father,

who takes me for a walk

on a fine fall day.

We watch the geese

flying far away.

They will come back

on a warm spring day.

Thank You, God,
for special times together,
when we talk about
Your love and care
and feel Your presence
everywhere.

Soon it will be Thanksgiving time
and everyone will sing,
''Thank You, God, for my family.
Thank You for everything.''

Thank You, God,
for the golden fields,
full of fluffy seeds
that float away . . .

like

tiny

puffy

parachutes

on a

windy

day.

Thank You, God,

for the silvery

squirrel,

for the leaves that twirl
as the autumn wind sings,

for the chipmunks
hunting seeds and things,

for special times together,
for fires warm and bright,

for my home, so warm and friendly
on a frosty moonlit night,

for geese flying miles across the sky,
saying goodby with a quack and cry.

Winter isn't far away.

Thank You, God, for a fine fall day.

Thanksgiving Day Is Coming

J.B.M.

Jane Belk Moncure

Thanks - giv - ing Day is com - ing, And ev - 'ry - one will sing,

"Thank You, God, for my fam - i - ly. Thank You for ev - 'ry - thing." Thanks-

giv - ing Day is com - ing, And ev - 'ry - one will say,

"Thank You for the friends I love. Hap - py Thanks-giv - ing Day!"